Holy Adventure

A Spiritual Memoir

Lynn Johnson MS

meetinghouse
newberg, or 97132

Holy Adventure
A Spiritual Memoir

Meetinghouse
Newberg, Oregon
https://www.meetinghouse.xyz/

Printed in the United States of America

Cover and page design: Mareesa Fawver Moss

Cover image: Moritz Knöringer

Author photo: Craig Norton

ISBN 978-1-59498-095-4

"...and when I heard it,
my heart did leap for joy."
—George Fox[1]

With love for my daughter, Lara,
and my granddaughters,
Anna, Lilli, and Ava.

With gratitude for the encouragement
and suggestions from Peterson, Paul,
Cruger, Lori, Millie, Joan,
Jann Dancing Wolf,
my sister Mary Keith, and detailed
memories from Elandara.

May you dwell happily in heaven;
Dad and Mom, Frederick, Dennis,

Bruce, and Gloria.
Thank you for all you taught me.

Seeking for the Light,
Life is holy adventure,
God in each flower.

Wilting Violet 1978, Lynn Johnson

Contents

In 1970, I asked a question of Elmer Brown, then executive secretary of Cambridge Friends Meeting in Massachusetts. "How do I know when to join and become a Quaker?" He answered me, "You don't become a Quaker; you discover you are one." I have been a member of the Religious Society of Friends since then; first in Cambridge, then New Haven, and now Hartford Monthly Meeting. Along the way, I have been clerk of New Haven Friends Meeting and Connecticut Valley Quarterly Meeting. I have served on worship and ministry committees, peace and social concerns and the green committee, and was endorsed in my ministry of pastoral counseling. I have clerked religious education and taught First Day school for many years. But what does it really mean to be Quaker? The answer does not come from our resumes of committees and works but from who we are. It is knowing the in-dwelling presence of God and seeing that of God everywhere. Here are stories of six different spiritual encounters I've had during my fifty years as a Friend. Some of them may seem unorthodox, but I have always been informed by the very light of Christ George Fox experienced almost 400 years ago.[2] I hope you will be inspired to seek and have your own holy adventures. For in this time of pandemic and our crisis of country and climate, we are still surrounded by God and beloved community.

I. Holy Laughter, 1972

I came to love Jesus when I was a little girl. My father read stories from the gospels to my sister and me when he put us to bed. As a teenager, I listened to the religious experiences of my friends. I felt disappointed that nothing spiritually dramatic happened to me.

I was wed and had a beautiful daughter named Lara, who truly opened my heart to love. However, I was failing in my marriage. I went home to my parents to pray and ask for help for what to do.

While there, I awoke one night in my childhood bed to the clear sound of laughter. I looked, but no one was there.

Frightened, I went to my parents' room, finding them asleep. I checked on Lara, who looked peaceful in her bed. Then I went to a window and saw lights in my friend Peggy's living room. I ran across the street in my bare feet and knocked. Peggy opened the door, surprised to see me in my nightgown.

"Lynn, what's wrong?"

"I hear laughter in my bedroom, and no one is there!" I shook as I spoke.

"What kind of laughter is it? Is it mean?" Peggy's clear blue eyes looked into my dark ones.

"Well—no." I thought about it. "It wasn't. It was a kind of loving laughter."

"Ahhh," Peggy smiled. "What was the laughter telling you?"

"Well—sort of like—everything is okay and not to worry," I slowly realized.

"Yes dear, you know who that is," she smiled again. "Go back to bed now; it's late. Goodnight!" She gently closed the door.

I walked back home, pondering what she had said.

Years later, I learned that this was a clairaudient experience.

The veil had been lifted.

We are never alone.

II. Holy Vision, 1978

I felt very intimidated. I had entered a workshop where everyone was a Yale art major, and my artistic ability was quite undeveloped. My Quaker friend, Paul had convinced me to go spend the day learning to draw with a man he greatly admired. Frederick Franck was a painter, sculptor, and author of many books on spirituality, including *The Zen of Seeing*.[3] He was a kindly looking older man, standing in front of me, explaining that I and the twenty other participants would now learn to see. "Seeing is the key to drawing," he explained. He would give us something to look at, and then we were to draw it. He walked around, placing different plants in each participant's hand. He gave me a leaf.

I stared at my maple leaf as hard as I could, then started to sketch. I wasn't pleased with how it was coming out. I heard Frederick going from student to student, commenting. "Ah, lovely!" and, "Yes, you are seeing!" Then he came to me. I waited, my face growing hot.

Frederick took my pencil from me, held my hand at the wrist and shook it. Then he put the pencil back in my hand. "Now try," he said.

My impulse was to run out of the room, but I didn't want everyone watching me. Embarrassed and discouraged, I looked down at my leaf and kept trying to draw. Tears slid down my face.

Frederick came back and said gently, "If you can get through this, you'll be able to see." He took the leaf out of my hand and placed a violet there instead.

I looked at the little violet in my hand. Hours had passed since Frederick had harvested the plant, so it had started to wilt. Through my tears, I felt that wilt. I started to draw.

Frederick came round again to look at my work, becoming excited at what he found. "You see the flower!" he exclaimed. He took away the violet and gave me a branch with many leaves. It looked huge to me.

Knowing I felt overwhelmed, he encouraged me.

"Expand your vision now! Feel the sweep of the branch, the movement of the leaves, and capture that!" He demonstrated a quick curving motion with my pencil.

I spent the final hours of his workshop drawing whatever he placed before me. Exhausted and exhilarated, I shook his hand and thanked him. I'm sure I wasn't the finest artist in his class, but I imagine I was the one who made the most progress.

Going outside, I was amazed at the world that greeted me. Everything sparkled! I saw each leaf on each tree clearly in focus.

In later years, I would remember what I saw when I read the words that Hildegard of Bingen wrote in the twelfth century, "There is no creation that does not have a radiance."[4]

The next morning was First Day, and still in a heightened state of awareness, I went to our Quaker meeting. We met in Connecticut Hall, inside the Yale Old Campus. The high-ceilinged room with its wooden floors and tall windows looked beautiful to me that day. The Friends sitting there were especially lovely. In silence, we sought the presence of the Divine. I usually had a hard time settling into worship, but then, I centered deep inside. I had the sensation of wilting, of my physical boundaries melting. Breathing slowly, I felt myself spreading into the room.

I spread out and touched each beloved Friend. I kept melting further, until I was outside in the courtyard. I was moving along the grass, touching the trees. I was part of everything.

When the end of meeting came, and we shook hands, it took some time for me to come back into my body. I looked around in wonder, my heart full of love. I will always remember that whole weekend and the miraculous sense of oneness I felt.

When I was studying at Yale Divinity School some years later, I read Evelyn Underhill's classic on mysticism. She would define what I experienced as a "unitive state."[5] Now, my heart hurts from all the damage we have done to our biosphere, plant, animal, and human life. I am called to spend my remaining days doing what I can to save God's earth and every inhabitant.

We are one with all creation.

III. Holy City, 1982

I awoke in a sweat, feeling exhausted. My nightmare was still vivid in my memory. It had begun pleasant enough; I was a girl living in a town where a dragon lived nearby. I had secretly befriended this dragon and frequently climbed the steep hill to his cave to visit with him.

I found him very beautiful, his scales sparkling a rainbow in the sunlight.

One day, my dragon went on a rampage. He roared down the hill to the bridge that crossed our river, burning the wooden structure with his breath. Flying into town, he knocked down buildings with his body, setting them on fire. I watched in horror and disbelief.

People were running and screaming as he finished his destructive path through the village, leaving it in rubble. He circled and then started back up to his cave. I ran after him, calling.

"Why did you do this? How could you destroy everything?"

He turned and looked at me sideways, through one glittering emerald eye. "I just lost control," he answered, strangely.

I ran back into town to see what I could do. Neighbors were bringing buckets of water from the river, dousing the fires. I saw my friend, Sharon, heavily pregnant and now in labor. She was searching for her husband, crying that she couldn't find him. Somewhere I found a blanket and a safe looking corner of a half-standing building and urged her to squat down. She was having the baby, and everyone around was busy putting out the fires, so there was no one to help us. I knew I had to assist in delivery, but I was panicked, and Sharon was screaming in pain.

I startled awake, disoriented. It took some time for me to calm down. Why did I have such a dream? This was one to take to my training group.

It was a circle of colleagues, New Haven psychotherapists, meeting monthly to learn to help our patients listen to the message of their dreams. We were training through sharing our own dreams with our facilitator Dennis Carney, a teacher of "Senoi Indian Dreamwork." This method was developed by anthropologist Kilton Stewart. Starting in 1934, Stewart began studying a tribe in the highlands of Malaya called the Senoi. He was intrigued with the marked peacefulness of this particular group of people, as contrasted with their neighbors. He concluded that the Senoi's different behavior was the result of their unique approach to dreams and dreaming. "This primitive educational system based on dream interpretation frees the mind of the adult Senoi from the type of rigidity on which crime, mental illness, and psychosomatic disease are now known to be predicated."[6] This education starts in childhood. "The Senoi parent inquires of his child's dream at breakfast, praises the child for having the dream, and discusses the significance of it."[7]

Children are taught that everything in the dream is their own creation, and with practice, they can transform nightmares into positive experiences. "The Senoi believes that any individual...can progressively master all of the forces of the spiritual world—the world of dreams and visions."[8]

I eagerly awaited my turn in the group to tell my dream to Dennis. I was surprised when he said it was a good dream. "But my dragon destroyed the whole village!" I demurred.

"Did he?" Dennis smiled. " I only heard he destroyed rigid structures, not anything living. Furthermore, your dream ends with a birth! Go back to your dragon in meditation, Lynn. He is a powerful part of you. Find out what he wants to teach you."

I mulled over those directions for weeks until one morning, in bed, when I was still half asleep. I decided, in my dreamlike state, to climb the hill to visit my dragon once more. I found him lying in his cave. Not knowing what to say, I sat quietly beside him. He opened one eye to gaze at me, then extended his tail and turned his head as if to tell me to climb up on his back. Hesitantly, I did so, until I found a comfortable place close to his head. He began to move out of his cave, and I held on tight. Much to my wonder, he lifted off and flew high up in the sky. It was simply heavenly near the clouds! The morning air was cool, but the warmth of the sun was on my face. I felt my dragon turn to the right and saw what looked like sparkling skyscrapers rising up from the clouds. Was I seeing the city of gold and jewels, the New Jerusalem of Revelation?[9]

As we flew toward the city, I realized I wasn't seeing buildings at all but giant radiant beings. As we went inside in between them, my dragon seemed as small as a bird, myself a tiny speck upon him. The beings brightly towered above me, emanating pure love. I felt I could reach out and touch each one. They seemed to bend and sway and smile toward us, blessing our presence with incredible peace. We floated through these glowing spirits, and I wanted to stay forever.

My ecstasy slowly faded, and I awoke in my bed, marveling at what I had seen. I know my vision was of the Holy City of Angels, a glimpse of the Divine. This experience of glory remains always in my memory.

It all felt so real!

Heaven is true.

IV. Holy Light, 1986

I was sure I had found my soulmate. We were studying *A Course in Miracles* together, my friend Ross and I, reading and practicing a lesson every few days. I thought he was the man I had been searching for, someone to join with me on my journey to deepen my faith and understanding. I was happy that I was in love with someone who was so attuned to his spirituality. He was tall and handsome, gentle and sensitive. I believed he returned my love.

But as time went by, Ross grew more and more distant with no explanation. Then, he just stopped coming over. I was very confused and hurt. What had I done that he would treat me this way?

What was wrong with me? I was devastated, in no small part because I had lost my study partner. The *Course in Miracles* is a challenging text, and I didn't want to tackle it alone. But as the weeks went by and he continued to ignore my calls, I realized he had disappeared from my life. Sadly, I knew I would have to continue on my own.

Determined to start again, I slammed the book down on my kitchen table one cloudy morning and went back to where we had stopped. We had reached Lesson 72.

"Holding grievances is an attack on God's plan for salvation."

The text instructed, "Ask what God's plan for us is."

"What is salvation, Father? I do not know. Tell me, that I may understand."[10]

Well, I certainly didn't understand! In my frustration, I prayed sincerely to be shown the meaning of salvation. Slowly, I sensed it grow lighter in the room. I turned to look out, but gray clouds still filled the sky. To the left of the window, a light was mysteriously growing.

I could discern the form of Christ being in the light, and I heard his clear answer to my prayer. *"Lynn, I am your salvation!"*

I was amazed and dumbfounded at what I heard, at the figure standing there, and at the stunning light that filled the whole floor of my house.

However, the light and the vision were surpassed in power by the love emanating from that light. I was enveloped in an all-embracing, all-accepting, all-affirming love, much beyond words. I understood that even though I was divorced, disorganized, a procrastinator, and sometimes foolish, it didn't matter to God.

I am beloved forever, just as I am.

I realized I had been looking for that kind of love from a man. I had finally found what I had been searching for, and I was full of joy. The paradox is that once I was free from the need of love from a man, it was given as a gift. I was to be married in a little more than a year after that life-changing experience.

The light slowly faded, but knowing I am loved and Christ's presence stay with me always.

We are loved for who we are.

V. Holy Mary, 1987

We were honeymooning on the Volga Peace Cruise. I was with Bruce, my beloved second husband, in the company of a group of American activists. It was a very exciting time for the people of the Soviet Union. Gorbachev had ushered in a period of *glasnost*, openness. At every town we visited, we were greeted by crowds of Russians with flowers and peace signs. We attended countless ceremonies calling for an end to the nuclear arms race. Although we were touched by these large gatherings, by the time we reached Leningrad, Bruce and I were growing weary of all the formalities. We longed for more everyday interactions. I wanted to attend church, which wasn't on the itinerary designed by the Soviet Peace Committee.

We quietly escaped our delegation after dinner on a Saturday night and entered the streets of Leningrad without a translator. We tried to buy a Soviet paper from an automatic dispenser, fumbling with our Russian coins. Obviously, we did not know what we were doing. A polite young man approached us and spoke in English, "May I help you?"

His name was Sergei, a Soviet in his twenties. He showed us how to get our paper. He stopped and talked with us about our trip and asked what more we wanted to see. When I explained that we wanted to find a church to go to on Sunday, his expression changed.

"Why do you want to do that?" He sounded disapproving.

"Well, we want a chance to worship with the Russian people." I watched Sergei, wondering about his response.

He was quiet for a moment. "We young people, we do not believe. My grandmother goes to Mass on Sunday. It is not a place for tourists. But if you like, I can take you there tomorrow."

We expressed our gratitude and agreed to meet in the morning.

The next day, Sergei joined us at our hotel and took us to the trolley, riding with us to the site of the church. It was a large yellow structure with scaffolding all around, as if in repair. Sergei went with us almost to the building, then stopped. "This is where I will leave you. There is the door where you go in. I don't want my grandmother to see me." He nodded to us, turned, and left. We never saw him again.

A bit unnerved by the sudden departure of our English-speaking companion, we walked through the doorway of the Russian Orthodox church. We had no idea what to expect. Our presence was not acknowledged as we entered a large room with a high gallery ceiling. The worshippers there were intent on the enormous icons all around, and they were lighting candles reverently. We followed the echoing sound of a voice into the next room. We found a priest robed in black, chanting Mass in a corner with his parishioners around him. There were no chairs that I remember. Not understanding his words, we wandered back into the room of icons. It was then that I saw her.

I stood entranced in front of one huge and particularly beautiful painting.

It was Mary but different than any of the other Marys in the room or of any other icon I had ever seen. The Madonna is usually portrayed holding the baby Jesus in her arms. But in the one before me, the child Jesus was a golden circle within her heart.

As I stared at the portrait, it dawned on me who Mary really is. She is the sacred union of the divine feminine and masculine. She is the embodiment of the light of Christ that George Fox wrote about in the seventeenth century.[11]

Not only did she birth Jesus as her child, but she held that light in her being. By her example, she asks us to let Christ be born in our own hearts. Deeply moved by this personal revelation, my tears flowed.

A small elderly woman in a headscarf approached me, speaking Russian. She pointed to my chest, then pointed to the icon. I had no idea what she was saying and could only shake my head. Another person joined her, then another. Soon there was a circle around me, trying to tell me something, pointing to my chest, and then to the icon. Bruce came over to support me but was just as bewildered as I. Blessedly, a woman appeared who spoke English. She explained that the Russian grandmother was devoted to this icon. She saw that I also loved Mary and wanted me to take her picture. Suddenly, I realized that a camera hung around my neck. It had become a part of me on our trip, and I had forgotten it was there. I remembered Sergei's words to us about not acting like tourists. "Oh no, I couldn't," I protested.

"It is perfectly alright," the English speaking lady assured me. "It would make her very happy."

"*Spasibo*," thank you. I used one of my few Russian words and smiled. She nodded and smiled back. I fumbled with my camera and somehow took a picture.

I was in a daze, so Bruce helped me through the crowd and out the door. I don't remember how we got back to the hotel. When I finally had my film developed, I was thrilled to see the precious icon appear among all the images. I treasure the photograph of Mary to this day. I will never forget what she showed me.

Love is the heart of our being.

VI. Holy Mystery, 2012

We were in the middle of our Magdalen Circle. Our group was drumming and singing, as we always did. Gloria Amendola, our leader, was in the middle of telling a story. I was distracted, hearing a voice that whispered, "Come away with me."

When I finally got home to where I could focus inside, the figure of Mary Magdalene appeared and spoke again. "Come with me." She took my hand and led me across the room. I looked up to see Jesus standing there. Mary sat down on the floor beside me. She patted the space next to her, gesturing that I should also sit. It was clear from this vision that she was telling me to take time to simply be with Jesus.

I greatly admire the Magdalen and the Madonna. They had the courage and devotion to stay at the cross with Jesus as he suffered and died, suffering together with their beloved.[12] Mary Magdalene was the first to greet him in his risen state.[13] I wanted to make a pilgrimage in her honor. Gloria led tours in France called the *Sacred Feminine,* to sites where Mary was said to have preached the gospel. As Margaret Starbird writes in *The Woman with the Alabaster Jar,* there is a town on the Mediteranean Coast called Saintes-Maries-de-la-Mer where it is recorded that Mary came by boat from the Holy Land, around 42 AD.[14] There is the round La Tour Magdala built in her memory, a tower in Rennes le Château. "In Hebrew, the epithet Magdala literally means 'tower' or…'magnificent.'"[15] And there is a cave (grotto) in the mountains of Sainte-Baume where Mary is said to have taken refuge at the end of her life.[16]

But I was not able to travel to France on pilgrimage. The symptoms of multiple sclerosis I developed over twenty years ago had progressed to where I was completely dependent on a walker. Traveling overseas was out of the question. Blessedly, there was somewhere closer I could go. In Rhode Island stood a mysterious old tower that some associate with Mary Magdalene. It was sacred to my friend and member of our circle, artist Elandara Anderson. She said we could go there together.

In August, we drove and stayed the weekend by the water in the beautiful city of Newport. We were excited to find the Newport Tower situated in a small city park with houses and a church surrounding. It is a large, round stone structure with a grass floor and open ceiling, twenty-eight feet high with three foot thick walls. It is supported by eight columns with arches in between, the mortar made from shells. It is known to have once been a windmill, and carbon dating says it was built around 1680. Many have thought it much older, as its structure compares with round towers built in medieval Europe. Most mysterious are the oddly spaced windows, which astronomers say align with stars and the summer solstice. It is a famous landmark of Newport and is used on ships' flags as its symbol.[17]

Elandara and I gazed at the tower with admiration, its impressive circular shape an inviting site for our pilgrimage. By honoring the sacred feminine as symbolized by Mary Magdalene, we sought to help restore the balance between male and female. "This restoration of the balance of opposites...(is) necessary for the well-being of civilization," says scholar and theologian Margaret Starbird. "The loss of the feminine has had a disastrous impact on our culture. Both male and female are deeply wounded...meanwhile the masculine continues to lead with his sword arm...often lashing out with violence and destruction."[18]

I had brought a many-faceted garnet crystal, its red the color associated with the Magdalen, to be placed for her within the tower. However, it was surrounded with an iron fence, chain locked at the gate. Elandara examined the chain where there was a small space between the lock and the gate and turned to me with a slightly mischievous smile. "I think we can crawl through this," she whispered.

We made our plans as we returned to our hotel. We would come back Friday at midnight to wiggle through and have a blessing ceremony inside. When we arrived, it was dark except for the floodlights illuminating the tower. Even though parked cars lined the side streets, we could see no one. I left my walker outside the gate and proceeded to crawl and squirm my way inside, following Elandara. The velvety black beauty of the night, the majestic columns, the soft grass, the stars shining down on us through the open roof—all were intoxicating. We began to laugh in spite of ourselves, shushing each other and peeking out to be sure no one heard us. I buried the garnet under a clump of grass in the center of the circle. We prayed and sang softly to the Sacred Feminine, seeking wholeness and healing for our planet.

We slept in late that Saturday after our early morning adventure. When we awoke, we knew we had to return to the tower. First, we went to the beach to find shells. I stayed in the car and waited, as rolling walkers do not work on sand. Elandara came back with thirteen quahog shells. (These are the shells from which Indigenous peoples made valuable beads called wampum.) Next, we searched for wildflowers. We went to three different beaches until we finally spotted a bush of rosa rugosa, a fitting symbol for Mary Magdalene. We picked several, finding a particularly lovely bloom for our largest shell. We planned to float the flowers in sacred water poured into the shells. Then we rested, dined, and waited for midnight to come.

When we arrived at the tower gate, we were surprised to see it slightly ajar and unchained! We wondered if someone had been watching us the night before and expected us back. We entered easily, and Elandara began placing our shells with their flowers in each of the four directions. We took care to tuck them under grass, very close to the columns. We wanted no one to see them from the outside. We placed our largest shell in the East, honoring Mary's homeland. Suddenly, we heard a rustling in the grass. Anxiously, we looked out to see a group of rabbits hopping around the tower. We felt much more subdued than the night before and didn't stay long after offering our gifts. We left, saying a prayer for peace and harmony on Earth, closing the gate behind us.

We awoke Sunday morning and had breakfast, packing up to check out of our hotel. Our plan was to go to our pilgrimage site to say goodbye, as we needed to get back home. But when we parked the car and looked over, we were amazed to see several people walking around inside the tower! Coming closer, we saw the gate swung wide open. Hesitating, we studied the people present to see if one of them appeared to be in charge. They were all gazing around in the hushed awe that the tower inspired. And there was something else different.

In the center of the grassy circle, right where I thought I had buried my garnet, stood a metal spike. It was approximately one inch in diameter with around four and a half feet protruding out of the ground. On top of the head of this giant nail perched our large shell with its deep pink flower still inside. Three of the smaller shells were placed on the grass in a circle around this sculpture. The spike and the rose created a symbol of the male and female!

We approached the spike carefully and tested to see if it was stable. It did not move. Clearly, it was driven deep into the ground—a feat of great strength and effort. Who had done this?

We started conversations with several other neighborhood visitors to the tower. None of them had seen anything unusual and hadn't found the tower unlocked before. We stayed as long as we could, hoping to discover more. No one who was in any official capacity appeared.

Our time in Newport had come to an end, as we had commitments to return to. We reluctantly got into Elandara's Prius and made our way back to Hartford, astounded at all that had happened. How had the chain been unlocked, and who created the symbol of the union of the sacred feminine and masculine? That remains a mystery, yet we knew intuitively that it was a man who responded to our prayer for the balance of masculine and feminine energy. Our invisible friend had left us a visionary message. The shell and the rose were elevated by the iron spike, the perfect symbol for gender harmony. Our offerings were understood and honored by a stranger who had the power to open the gate.

In our hearts, we knew this person was the keeper of the tower, though we never learned his name. We will always be grateful for him and for that holy adventure.

In this time of great turbulence, sexism, racism and violence, we need to know that love and harmony prevail.

In truth, we are one.

Seen and unseen, the beloved community surrounds us!

Icon, Russian Orthodox church,
Leningrad, USSR, 1987
Photo by Lynn Johnson

Lessons from the Holy

We are never alone.
We are one with all creation.
Heaven is true.
We are loved for who we are.
Love is the heart of our being.
Seen and unseen, the beloved community
surrounds us.

Addendum:
How to Have Holy
Adventures

Holy adventures cannot be planned, but they can be sought.

"Keep on seeking, and you will find" (Matthew 7:7 NLT).

"...blessed are your eyes, because they see; and your ears, because they hear" (Matthew 13:16 NLT).

- Holy adventures come through seeking.

- Holy adventures come through adversity.

- Holy adventures come through nature.

- Holy adventures come through dreams.
- Holy adventures come through people.
- Holy adventures come through grace.
- Holy adventures come through seeing and hearing with the heart.

Go and seek your own holy adventures!

"The Light Within," commissioned by LJ,
painted by Elandara, 2013

Bibliography

The following books and article have profoundly affected my spiritual journey.

Fox, George. *The Journal of George Fox.* Richmond, Indiana: Friends United Press, 1976.

Franck, Frederick. *The Zen of Seeing.* New York: Vintage Books, 1973.

Beyond Suffering Bible. New Living Translation. Carol Stream, Illinois: Tyndale House Publishers, 2016.

Schucman, Helen. *A Course in Miracles: A Workbook for Students.* Tiburon, CA: Foundation for Inner Peace, 1975.

Starbird, Margaret. *The Woman with the Alabaster Jar.* Santa Fe, New Mexico: Bear and Co., 1993.

Stewart, Kilton. "Mental Hygiene and World Peace" *Mental Hygiene* 38, 1954. 387–407.

Uhlein, Gabriele. *Meditations with Hildegard of Bingen.* Santa Fe, New Mexico: Bear and Co., 1983.

Underhill, Evelyn. *Mysticism.* New York: New American Library, 1974.

Endnotes

1 Fox, George. The Journal of George Fox (Richmond, IND, 1976), p.82.

2 Fox, p. 101.

3 Franck, Frederick, *The Zen of Seeing* (New York, 1973), p. 9.

4 Uhlein, Gabriel, *Meditations with Hildegard of Bingen,* (Santa Fe, New Mexico, 1983)*,* p.52.

5 Underhill, Evelyn. *Mysticism* (New York, 1974), p. 81.

6 Stewart, Kilton, "Mental Hygiene and World Peace" *Mental Hygiene* 38, 1954. p. 391.

7   Stewart, p. 396.

8   Stewart, p 395.

9   *Holy Bible*. Revelation 21:18–21.

10 Schucman, Helen. *Course in Miracles Workbook* (Tiburon, CA, 1975), p. 122-123.

11 Fox, p. 101.

12 *Holy Bible.* John 19:25.

13 *Holy Bible.* John 20:1–18.

14 Starbird, Margaret. *The Woman with the Alabaster Jar* (Santa Fe, New Mexico, 1993), p. 60.

15 Starbird, p.51.

16 "Sainte-Baume." *Wikipedia.* Retrieved January 18, 2021, from https://en.wikipedia.org/w/index.php?title=Sainte-Baume&oldid=965525582

17 "Newport Tower (Rhode Island)." *Wikipedia*. Retrieved January 18, 2021, from https://en.wikipedia.org/w/index.php?title=Newport_Tower_(Rhode_Island)&oldid=9944348

18 Starbird, p. XXII.

www.ingramcontent.com/pod-product-compliance
Lightning Source LLC
Chambersburg PA
CBHW051434090426
42737CB00014B/2966